Digging
挖

Ren Yi

任意

Translated by Ouyang Yu

译者：欧阳昱

PUNCHER & WATTMANN

First published in 2020
Published by Puncher and Wattmann
PO Box 279
Waratah NSW 2298

http://www.puncherandwattmann.com
puncherandwattmann@bigpond.com

**NATIONAL
LIBRARY**
OF AUSTRALIA

A catalogue entry for this book is available from the National Library of
Australia.

ISBN   9781925780819

Printed by Lightning Source International

Contents

75 poems by Ren Yi

Ren Yi, whose real name is Ren Zhilin, born in the 1950s, is from Shanghai. He is now deputy secretary-general of the Pujiang Literature Society, deputy general manager of Pujiang Literature Exchange Centre for Literature and Arts, Minhang, Shanghai, and an editor of *Pujiang Literature*.

睛镶玉

想起那年
金子八十元一克
我在中英街
买了个戒指三百六

被罚税四十
我问同行
他们买了好几千都没罚
时距离境还有两钟头

把我气得
戴着戒指去电影院
看了部 III 级片
把叶玉卿

张曼玉
梁思敏、李丽珍
一个个玉体
镶进眼睛

Eyeballs Embedded with Jade

I remember I bought a ring for 360
Eighty dollars per gram, of gold
In Chinese-English Street
That year

I got fined for forty
But when I checked with my colleagues
They all said they had bought stuff for thousands of dollars without being fined
It was only two hours before we departed

I was so angry
I went to the cinema wearing the ring
And saw a porn film
Embedding the bodies of

Maggie Cheung
Ivy Leung and Loretta Lee
In my eye
Balls III

一百斤煤屑

爸爸从好几个朋友家里
筹到一百斤煤屑
从四十公里外用自行车往家驮
早上六点出门
晚上八点还没到家
我等不及先睡了
第二天我问
爸爸昨晚啥时回来的
他笑了笑："哎——
昨天到半路
发现麻袋破了
停下自行车
循着洒在路上的煤屑
寻回去足有三百米
我用手一点点扫起来
放进中山装
两只大袋袋里
又脱下袜子
塞了麻袋漏洞
到屋里已经半夜了"
这是一九八六年
弄到一百斤煤屑不容易
爸爸借来大秤复称
结果称到了
一百十五斤

A Hundred *Jin* of Coal Dust

After he managed to scrape together a hundred *jin*
Of coal dust from a number of his friends
Dad rode his bike home with the dust, from 40 kilometres away
He had started out at 6am
But had not arrived home by 8pm
I couldn't wait, I went to bed
The next day I asked him
What time he came back last night
He smiled: 'Well---
Yesterday when I was halfway
I found the gunny sack had a hole in it
I stopped my bike
And traced the coal dust on the road
For a full three hundred meters
I swept it all up, with my hands
And put it in the two big pockets
Of my Mao Suit
And took off my socks
Stuffing the hole with them
When I arrived home it was past midnight'
That was 1986
It wasn't easy to get 100 *jin* of coal dust
Dad borrowed a big steelyard to weigh it again
And what he got was
115 *jin*

墙上的钉子

老屋墙上一枚钉子
挂过父亲的草帽和镰刀
也挂过母亲捆柴禾的草绳

几十年了 这枚钉子
仍然银光铮亮
如今 挂着母亲的孤独与忧伤

当年父亲钉这枚钉子
是为了挂我的书包
想挂起一家人的希望

他从未想过
哪天会把自己挂在
墙上

The Nail on the Wall

Father's straw hat and sickle
As well as Mother's straw rope that had tied the bundle of firewood
Have hung on a nail on the wall of the old house

Despite the passage of decades   this nail
Remains shiny, like silver
Now, Mother's loneliness
And sorrow is hanging on it

In the old days when Father nailed it in
He meant for it to hang my school sachet
To hang the hope
Of the whole family

It has never occurred to him, though   that one day
He'll hang himself
On the wall

挖

妻子坐在田地里挖
我坐在田埂上挖

妻子挖红薯
我挖诗

妻子稍一挖
就挖出一个红薯

我挖老半天
才挖出一行句子

妻子越挖越得意
我越挖越失意

妻子挖过的红薯地
一行一行　有长有短
起起伏伏像一首诗

我挖出的诗
每一行都疙疙瘩瘩
像地壁虎咬过的红薯

Digging

Squatting, my wife was digging in the field
While I was digging, sitting on the ridge

My wife was digging for the sweet potatoes
And I was digging for poetry

With an easy dig
My wife dug out a sweet potato

But I spent a long time
Managing to dig out only a single line

The more my wife dug the more delighted she was
But the more I dug, the more frustrated I was

The field where my wife had dug for the sweet potatoes
Had furrows, long and short
Meandering like lines of poetry

Whereas the poems I had dug
Had each line so knotty
That it resembled the sweet potato, gnawed by the ground lizard

回家

每年春节回家
他都要几天几夜地
排队买火车票
又总买不到

今年春节是由
两名警察陪他回来的
还免了火车费二百八十元
汽车费六十元 饭钱三十元
坐黑车钱十元

村长从车站接他回家后
又送了一千元慰问金
乡长也拨了二千元扶贫款

父亲问：你在北京当官啦？
他说：我还在工地抹灰
父亲说：这回你真给家里长脸
他却扑簌簌地落泪

从随身的编织袋里拿出
一条写着"我要上访"的红布
跪在父亲面前说：我错了
父亲什么再没说

Coming Home

Each year when he comes home on Spring Festival
He'll spend days and nights in a queue
Trying in vain
To buy a train ticket

Last Spring Festival, however
He was escorted home by two policemen
Bar the 280 yuan for the train
60 yuan for the bus   30 yuan for the meals
and 10 for an unlicensed cab

When the head of the village met him and took him home
He gave him one thousand yuan as a comfort fee
And the head of the town, too, gave him two thousand yuan as part of the relief
       fund

Father said: Have you become an official in Beijing?
He said: I'm still working as a plasterer in the construction site
Father said: You are bringing so much credit to your family now!
He was in tears

From a braided bag he had with him
He pulled out a red cloth, written with 'I want to petition!'
And was on his knees before his father, saying: I've done wrong
His father said no more

雷雨中

那天有雷
我在暴雨中赶路

把泼在彩钢板上的雨
听成了机枪的扫射

把黄浦江
看成了大渡河

将远处闵浦大桥斜拉杆
看成了晃动的铁索

将阵阵闷雷
听成了手榴弹炸

将晃眼闪电
看成了 22 名红军背上的大刀

Amidst the Rain and Thunder

There was thunder the other day
And I was hurrying along in the thunderous rain

The rain pouring on the colour steel plates
Sounded like the strafing of the machine-gun fire

The Huangpu River
Looked like the Dadu River

The diagonal cross braces of the Min-Pu Bridge in the distance
Looked like the swaying iron chains

Peals of simmering thunder
Sounded like the blasting of hand grenades

And the blinding flashes of lightning
Looked like the broadswords on the backs of the 22 Red Army soldiers

绑树

台风过后
村前一排新栽树一致倒向右边
我拿出绑带和木棍
把它们扶正绑牢
我在做这些的时候
传来走路声音
先是拖沓的，好像很吃力
后是急促的，有点凌乱
再后的很整齐很雄壮
环顾四周没有队伍经过
我继续绑树 却发现
有一根绑带绑在自己腿上
这让我想起 曾经有一群人
是绑着腿走路的
他们打着绑腿穿着草鞋
走了许多路 走出了
一条自己想走的路

Tying the Trees Up

After the typhoon
The row of newly planted trees in the village had all fallen to the right
I propped them and tied them up in a secure position
With the binding bands and wooden sticks
While I was doing this
I heard the footsteps
Sluggish, and laborious
Then they became hurried, a little disorderly
Before the order set in when the sound turned majestic
I looked around but found no troops
I kept tying the trees up when I found
I had tied one band around my own leg
Which reminded me of   a group of people
Who had once walked with tied-up legs
With leg wrappings and in straw shoes
They'd walked many roads, treading
A road that they had wanted to tread on

情人节那天

"说过两天就来
已一星期仍不见你影
今天是情人节，我边摸
自己被你吮过
无数次的乳房边
手淫
中指没你那个粗，总是
达不到高潮
你走的那天说过
不让打电话不让发短信
可就是忍不住
现在我裹紧你的浴袍
想象你压在我身上
快来吧
我的阴户只为你开"

她翻身把他骑在胯下
问：这个爱你的丽丽住在哪里？

On Valentine's Day

'You said you'd come in two days
but I haven't seen you for a week
it's Valentine's Day today. As I touch
my breasts that you've sucked
countless times I
masturbate myself
my middle finger not as thick as yours, which is why
I never reach an orgasm
the day you left you said
not to call nor text
but I just can't help it
now, wrapped tightly in your bathing gown, I
imagine you on me
come quick
as my vagina is open only for you'

she was turning over and riding on him
saying, 'Where is this Lili that you are in love with?'

礼拜天

耶稣在教堂
墙上受难

门口 那些忏悔爱子
人贯而入

一白面镜男
在默读招聘广告

几只鸽子
盯着他手上面包

Sunday

Jesus in the church
Is suffering on the wall

At the entrance   those confessing Christians
Are entering in a single file, like real people

A white-faced man with spectacles
Is reading an advertisement for recruitment

While a number of doves
Are staring at the bread in his hand

穿针

老婆在太阳下
缝被子
穿了半天
那个线头怎么穿
也穿不进针眼
让我帮忙

我刚举起针
一只飞机穿了过去

Threading the Needle

My wife, in the sun
Was sewing a quilt
She spent a long time
Trying to thread the needle
But in vain
She was asking me for help

Just as I raised the needle
A plane went through its eye

擦

早上重霾
看不清去路
用纸巾擦了擦
眼睛
擦掉了
地上一只鸟
擦出了
天边
三声狗叫

Wiping

A heavy haze in the morning

So heavy I couldn't see the road before me

I wiped my eyes

With a tissue

Wiping out a bird

On the ground

Till

A dog barked three times

At the edge of the sky

闪电

是位外科医生
在宇宙
这张手术台上
把天空的胸腔打开
又迅即缝合

The Lightning

was a surgeon
and, on the operating table
of the universe
he opened the chest of the sky
before it, swiftly, sewed it up

怀念一棵树

一棵八百多年的银杏树
我与她已分别整半个世纪

前天去大治河边看她
未见其粗壮身影

但我相信她一定还在
如果站着

定是某处一道风景
如果躺着

可能是条板凳
一张讲台

也许是僧人禅房的木鱼
文人书房的扁额

或者正搁着哪个老板
精致的茶具

如果有幸做成了骨灰盒
恳求一定给我留一只

这样我们就可以
永不分离

Missing a Tree

A gingko tree, more than eight hundred years old
But I have been living in separation from her for a whole half-century

The day before yesterday I went to the Dazhihe River to see her
But I didn't see her thick body

I, though, believe that she is still there
If she stands

She must be the landscape of a certain place
And if she lies down

She may be a bench
Or a podium

Or a Buddhist wooden fish
Or a horizontal tablet over the study of a man of letters

Or a tea table on which sits
A businessman's delicate teacup

If, fortunately, she is turned into a box of bone ashes
Please do keep one for me

So we shall never
Be separated again

邻里关系

每年去福乐山庄
给父亲扫墓
烧锡箔

妈妈总会提醒
给隔壁阿姨
也烧一点

你爸爱叉麻将
出去后万一下雨
让她帮忙收收衣服

A Neighbourly Relationship

Every year I go to Happy and Pleasant Mountain Village
And sweep the grave of my father
And burn the tinfoil paper

Mother always reminds me
To burn a few pieces
For the aunty next door

Saying: Dad loves playing Mahjong
If it happens to rain
She'll help get in the laundry

杀鸽子

菜场外有许多人在
围观杀鸽子

一只只鸽子
被一只戴方戒的手

卡住脖子活活闷死
然后褪毛开膛

一位老阿姨直呼
"作孽，作孽

这是一条条命啊
也有灵魂的"

一位老爷叔瞟了瞟她
"这年头

人们只想着吃肉
哪顾得上灵魂"

Killing the Doves

Outside the vegetable market, many were watching
The killing of doves

One dove after another
Was strangled alive

By a hand wearing a square ring
Before it was disembowelled, with feathers removed

When an old aunty cried
'Sin, sin

They are lives
And they have souls'

An old man glanced at her
'These days

People think of only eating the flesh
And who gives a damn about the soul'

看

我坐在公园的长椅上看书
不断有人坐到身边
左边 右边 右边 左边
被挤得无法翻书
只好站起来
我看了看这些人
发现都是男人
两个是年轻人
一个是中年人 还有一个
头发已经白了
他们略低着头看着对面
对面有一个女人
穿着裙子靠在椅子上看手机
她两腿叉开 露出雪白的大腿
从大腿看上去 中间一块
粉红色 凹凸有致
有人反复在她对面走过去
又走过来 我离开时
那女孩还在看手机

Looking

I was sitting on a park bench, reading
People kept coming and sat by my side
On the left   on the right   on the right   on the left
I was so squeezed I couldn't turn a page
So I stood up
When I had a look I saw
All of them were men
Including two young men
One middle-aged man   and one
Whose hair had turned grey
Their heads all slightly lowered, looking at the opposite side
Where there was a woman
In a skirt, reclining on a chair, looking at her mobile phone
Her legs opened   revealing snow-white legs
If you looked between them   you could see an evenly
Bulging place   pink
Someone repeatedly walked past her, to
And fro   when I left
The girl was still looking at her phone

时事

天光微茫
街边公园很盲
树林里有女声在练唱
"我身骑白马走三关"
字正腔不圆
一白发老者
左手拎半瓶水
右手握长杆毛笔
在石阶上写
"何时缚住苍龙"
酱红步道间
有人前行有人倒走
一高个戴着听诊器
匆匆而来
我想：这个没穿
白大褂的医生
莫非要去哪里出诊
走近才看清他
耳朵塞的是入耳式耳机
有一只耷拉在左耳边
一根线垂向右口袋

我们相向而过
听见一个模糊男声
"马克龙说
勒庞传谣
我要诉诸法律"

Current events

The light of the sky was dim
The street-side park, blindly busy
A woman's voice practicing singing in the woods
'I'm riding a white horse to pass through the three passes'
Good words, bad tunes
A white-haired man
Half a bottle of water in his left hand
And a long-stemmed brush in his right
Was writing on a stone step
'I wonder when I shall bind up the Black Dragon'
On the dark-red path
Someone was stepping forwards, someone was stepping backwards
A tall man wearing a stethoscope
Was hurrying along
I thought: Is this doctor
Not in white going to see a patient in his home?
When he got near, I saw
Him wearing an earphone, his ear stuffed
Another one hanging by his left ear
With a string drooping towards his right pocket

Face to face, we went past each other
As I heard an indistinct male voice
'Macron said
That Le Pen was spreading the rumour
I'll resort to the law'

傍晚

远远看见一个篮球
正落进篮筐
走近球场
发现里面根本没人打球
只是天正渐渐暗下来

Towards the evening

I saw, from a distance, a basketball
Was falling into a basket
When I got near the basketball court
I found that there was no one there
Except that the day was, gradually, darkening

两个黑人

北京时间 13 点
人挤人的上海地铁
2 号线这会不挤
坐位上有人看手机
有人闭目打盹
站的人在地铁的晃动中摇晃
江苏路站上来 2 个黑人
1 个是高个男
另 1 个也是男高个
1 个背旅行包
另 1 个耳麦传出迈克杰克逊
You are not alone
到南京东路站
背包黑人在 1 个空位上坐下来
不停挪动屁股
旁边那女人不得不站起来
他侧身让耳麦坐到旁边
伸出长长白舌头舔他黑鼻子
耳麦配合地也伸出白舌头
他们不避周遭目光
滑向凳沿把手伸向对方裤裆
晃荡的车厢正好配合着他们挖抓节奏
两根舌头肉搏声
没有盖过地铁咣当
到世纪大道站
他们手牵手下了车

Two black men

At 1 p.m. Beijing time
In the Shanghai subway where people were crowding people
No. 2 not so crowded at the moment
Someone, seated, was looking at his mobile phone
Someone was taking a nap
Those standing swayed from side to side with the sway of the subway
2 black men came in at Jiangsu Road
1 a tall man
Another 1 also a tall man
1 carrying a backpack
Another 1 with an earphone playing Michael Jackson
'You are not alone'
At Nanjing East Station, the backpacked man sat down in 1 vacant seat
He kept moving his buttocks
So the woman next to him had to stand up
He sidled over for the earphoned man to sit next to him
Sticking out a long white tongue to lick his black nose
They, not trying to avoid the glances shot their way
Slid to the edge of their seats, their hands extended to each other's crotch
The swaying compartment matching the rhythm of their grabbing and digging
The sound of their tongue-to-tongue combat
Wasn't loud enough to drown the din of the subway
At Century Avenue
They got off, hand in hand

同机

右边一个是白人
还有一个也是白人
他们戴着眼罩
靠在椅背上
再右边是舷窗
和舷窗外一团团白云

左边是过道
过道的左边坐着
两位长发青年
一个用纤细手指
点了一下对方额头
一个用绵软的掌
摸着对方白净脸颊
被乘务长阻止

我问：她们怎么了
有人反映她们举止不雅
我说：她们没有大声喧嚷
也没有不堪入眼举动
如她们是异性你会干预吗
乘务长：她们是——
本想骂：你这没人性的东西
却只说了句：为什么不让同性
享受同一种目光呢
乘务长说：同性恋太恶心了

长发同时站起

两个嗓音一粗一细
谁说我们是同性恋

In the same plane

On the right side, there was also a white man
And there was another one, also a white man
Their eyes covered with blinkers
They sat leaning against the back of the chair
Further on the right side was the porthole
And masses of cloud outside it

The aisle was on the left side
On the left side of the aisle sat
Two long-haired young women
One pointed at the forehead of the other
With her slender finger
Another touched the white and clean cheek of the other
With her soft palm
But this was stopped by the chief attendant

I said: But why?
She said: People are complaining about their inelegant behaviour
I said: But they're not making any noise
Nor are they doing anything ugly that offends the eye
Would you intervene if they are man and woman?
The chief attendant: But they are—
I was on the point of saying: You are inhuman
Instead, I said: Why don't you let the gays and lesbians
Enjoy the same way people look at people?
The chief attendant said: They are so disgusting

The long hairs stood up

Their two voices, one thick, the other thin

Saying: Who says we are gays?

捉迷藏

丁酉年正月十三上午
有首诗与我躲猫猫
总是抓不住
而今春第一场雪
也似游魂在太阳下东躲西闪
我想看看这冷与暖
怎样让对峙的天地言和
刚到室外却不见了影
只有发抖的风
从袖口和脖颈伸进手来
想盗走我身体的暖
这时我似捉到了诗
回屋拿起笔诗却再次开溜
雪又在飘
再次来到室外，却又已无踪

Hide and seek

On 9th February, in the Year of Dingyou (2017)
A poem was playing cat-cat (peek-a-boo) with me
I found it hard to catch
And the first snow of this spring
Was also hiding here and there, like a roaming soul
I wanted to see how this coldness and warmness
Made peace between earth and heaven, pitted against each other
But as soon as I went outdoors I didn't see a shadow of it
Except the trembling wind
That got its hand in my sleeves and around my neck
Intending to steal the warmth from me
It's not till then that I seemed to have caught the poem
But it slipped away when I got back into the house
The snow started floating again
When I went outside, it's gone, without a trace

我家有个金不换

换好新电脑后
我说现在家里只剩一样
还没换
老婆扫了一遍
冰箱洗衣机电饭锅电视机
空调大衣柜和床
问：哪个没换
我说：老婆还没换
没想到她说
"如果你觉得不好用
也换一个"

I have someone priceless at home

After the old computer was replaced with the new
I said that there was only one item
That was not changed
My wife glanced across
The fridge, the washing machine, the rice cooker and the TV
The air-con, the wardrobe and the bed
And said: What is it?
I said: The wife
Unexpectedly, she said
'If you don't think it's useful
You can also replace it'

正月十五

家里人都到城隍庙
看灯去了

住在城隍庙附近的
孃孃特意开车

赶来乡下
我问怎么不去看灯

她抬头自语
嗯，这乡下的月

还真比城里
的亮

15th January

All my family turned out and went to the Chenghuang Temple
To watch the lanterns

Niang Niang, my aunty, who lived close to it
Went out of her way in a car

To the country
When I asked why she didn't go and see the lanterns

She said, to her self, as she raised her head
Well, the moon in the country

Was really brighter than the moon
In the city

帽子

二大爷一生
戴过许多帽子
瓜皮帽
礼帽
六个角的绒帽
臭老九帽
反革命帽
还戴过一段时间绿帽
破草帽
死了以后
二大娘给他戴了
顶鸭舌帽

Hats

All his life, my second grandfather

Has worn many a hat

A melon hat

A top hat

A 6-cornered cashmere cap

A stinking-ninth hat

An anti-revolutionary hat

A green hat, for a while[1]

And a torn straw hat

After his death

His wife put on his head

A duck-tongue hat

---

1 A green hat, or 绿帽子 , in Chinese, is a euphemistic reference to someone being cuckolded – translator's note.

爸——爸

父亲一生
从未在当面听我
叫过一声爸爸
在世时我一直叫他爷叔
工作后曾发誓要改口
可一见面
心里叫的是爸爸
嘴里出来的还是爷叔

当我终于改口时
父亲已听不见
那天夜里
我拼命摇他身体
不停地叫
爸爸 爸——爸
爸爸
却一直没有应答

负罪六十年
今天终于释怀
就在刚才
看见一个推三轮车
卖炒货白发老头
我叫爸爸时
隔空中传来了一声
哎——

Daaa---d

In his entire life, father
Never heard me call him Father
In his presence
After he died, I always called him Yeshu[2]
When I got a job, I swore that I'd change that
But as soon as I met him
Yeshu came out of my mouth
Although I had called him Dad at heart

Eventually when I made the change
Father wasn't able to hear it
That night
I shook his body hard
And I kept calling
Dad   daaa---d
But dad
Never replied

This sense of guilt lasted 60 years
Till today
When I saw a white-haired old man
Pushing a wheelbarrow
And selling the roasted nuts and seeds just now
I called out, 'Dad'
And a voice answered in the air
Oh, yeh—

---

2 Or 爷 叔 , a Shanghai colloquialism about one's father's brothers – the
translator's note.

目击

你信吗？
几十条生命
被一口吞噬

院门外
一群蚂蚁
正在搬运一小块
小鲜肉

一只黄狗跑来
汪了几声
一只黑猫
主动退出战斗

黄狗用右前爪
拨了两下小鲜肉
把它们全吞了
连骨头也没吐出来

Bearing witness

Do you believe
that scores of lives
were swallowed in one mouthful?

Outside the courtyard
a group of ants
was moving a small morsel
of fresh meat

when a yellow dog came running over
and barked a few times
before a black cat
offered to back out of the battle

the yellow dog, twice, turned the meat over
with his right front paw
and swallowed it up
without even spitting out the bone

问候

在上海某医院蹭空调
看见取药窗口
屏幕上跳出一个
熟悉的名字
我给他打电话
人却在兰州
于是顺便问他
"你老毛病好点了吗"

Greetings

In a Shanghai-based hospital, I freely availed myself of the air-con there
When I saw a familiar name
Jump onto the screen
Above the Dispensing Window
I followed it up with a phone call
But he was in Lanzhou
So I just said
'How's your old condition, getting better now?

春阳里

右手中指食指拇指
将一撮烟叶渣
放到左手一张狭长的
黄草纸上卷住
又放在左腿上用右手心
不停地往前搓
在地铁8号线沈杜路站外
这些熟悉的动作
竟让我看到了父亲
他坐在花坛石上
认真地卷烟
父亲烟瘾很大
凭票火柴不够用
去世后
每年扫墓时我会在
父亲墓碑上点三支烟
留一盒火柴
现在火柴盒又空了
我走过去一边用打火机
给他点烟一边拨掉
粘在白胡子上的饭粒
留下半包软中华

In the spring sunshine

The index finger, the middle finger and the thumb of the left hand
Were putting a pinch of tobacco residue
On a narrow piece of yellow grass paper in the left hand
Before rolling it up
And continuously twisting and rubbing it back and forth
In the heart of the right hand on the left leg
Outside Shendu Road Station on the Subway Route No. 8
These familiar movements
Caused me to see my father:
He was sitting on a stone in the flower bed
Seriously rolling a cigarette
He was heavily addicted
And never had enough coupons for matches
After his death
When I do the annual tomb-sweeping I'll
Light up three cigarettes on his grave
And leave a box of matches there
Now, the box is empty again
I walk over, lighting up his cigarettes
With a lighter as I flipped off a grain of rice
Stuck on his white beard
And put down half a packet of soft *Chunghwa*

犯人

1958 年 11 月
他正闷着从大便里
捡出未消化的麦子
看见许多人
在排队领馒头
乘人不意
闷声混进队伍
刚拿到馒头
就被一个端枪的人
推上闷罐车
从宝鸡带到了德令哈
闷头闷脑闷进
架着电网的高墙后
就彻底闷了
40 年后有人公开
他的遗书

"……今夜只有戈壁
草原尽头是青海劳改农场
我两手颤抖
悲痛时握不住
一个馒头……"

The prisoner

In November 1958
While he was, quietly, picking up wheat, undigested
From the excrement
He saw many forming a queue to receive their steamed bread
In an unexpected move
He quietly mixed with the queue
But as soon as he got his bread
He was pushed onto a tank car
By a man carrying a gun
Taken from Baoji to Delingha
Quietly entering
Behind the tall wall with electrical wiring
And going thoroughly quiet
It was not till 40 years after
That his letter was made public:

'...tonight there is only the Gebi Desert
And at the end of the grassland is the Qinghai Labour Camp
My hands trembling, I was
So sad I could hardly
Hold a bread steady...'

在畜牲面前

我总是不待见

比如邻居家这狗
张三路过不叫
李四逗它不叫
王五踢它不叫
赵六抽它不叫
我一出现
就猛扑上来
汪个不停

即使曾给它喂过肉

Before the animals

They never like to see me

Take our neighbour's dog
He doesn't bark when Zhang Three goes past
He doesn't bark when Li Four teases him
He doesn't bark when Wang Five kicks him
He doesn't bark when Zhao Six whips him
But as soon as I appear
He pounces on me, with a vengeance
Barking without stop

Even if I fed him once

奶奶和鲁迅及酱和奖

其实，奶奶与鲁迅没有半毛关系，只是奶奶会做酱，鲁迅善用酱，这才有了点牵扯。

现在人们用肉做肉酱，用鱼做鱼酱，用果做果酱，用辣椒做辣椒酱。记得奶奶曾用小麦粉做甜面酱，用豆子做豆瓣酱；读书后发现，鲁迅很会用酱。

他借高尔础口说："我辈正经人，确乎犯不上酱在一起……"，又在致胡风信谈萧军是否参加左联时说："一到里面去即酱在无聊的纠纷中"。于是有人就用鲁迅做了奖。

吃过奶奶的甜面酱，豆瓣酱，偶尔也吃点辣椒酱，某日突想鲁奖，上网一查，确乎已停奖。

Grandma and Lu Xun and Jam and the Awards[3]

In fact, Grandma has nothing to do with Lu Xun at all except that Grandma is good at making paste or sauce and Lu Xun, eating it, which somehow relates one to the other.

People now make meat sauce with meat, fish sauce with fish, fruit jam with fruit and chili sauce with chili. I remember when I was little, Grandma would make sweet flour paste with wheat flour or thick broad-bean sauce with beans. When I went to school, I found that Lu Xun was a very good eater of all sorts of sauce.

He quoted Gao Erchu to say, 'We are all decent people and don't have to mix together like jam...' and, in a letter to Hu Feng, discussing whether Xiao Jun had joined the League of Left-wing Writers, he said, 'as soon as one joins it one gets into the boring entanglement like jam'. As a result, an award was named after Lu Xun.[4]

After I had Grandma's sweet flour sauce and broad-bean sauce, I sometimes feel like having a bit of chili sauce. One day, I had a sudden thought that I should go for the Lu Xun Award. But as soon as I went online and checked, the award had surely been terminated.

---

3 The English words, 'sauce, paste and jam', can all be represented in one Chinese word, 酱 (jiang) - the translator's note.

4 The English word, 'award', is pronounced exactly the same as the Chinese word, 酱 (jiang) , 'sauce, paste or jam' - the translator's note

改名

高干亭改名高尔础
藉以和高尔基攀亲
尽管连高尔基是否姓高
也云里雾里
鲁迅死后
高尔础逐亡
随着高考中考毕
一些学生家长
有动于衷
让高尔础活了起来
少则 500 元多
则 1000 元
为孩子改名转运气
一所大学一个班
有十几个高升
为区别
老师只得叫
大高升
小高升
胖高升
瘦高升
矮高升
高高升

Name-changing

Senior-cadres Pagoda changed its name to Gao Erchu

So they can somehow get related to Gao Erji (Gorky)

Even though one is not sure whether Gorky

Is really surnamed Gao (high)

After Lu Xun died

Gao Erchu gradually died away

With the high school graduates going for the entrance examination

A number of parents

Moved enough by profit-making

Revived Gao Erchu

They changed their kids' names

For 500 yuan at its lowest

Or 1000 yuan at its maximum

As name-changing for kids would bring in good luck

With the result that there were more than a dozen

Who had ascended to a university class

To distinguish them

The teacher had to call them

Big Ascendant

Small Ascendant

Fat Ascendant

Thin Ascendant

Short Ascendant

Tall Ascendant

放不下

心里多年
放不下你
但没想好
该放哪里
珠穆朗玛
怕有雪崩
扔太平洋
又怕海啸

Un-put-downable

For many years
You have been
un-put-downable
in my heart
and I have
not worked out
where to put
you down if
I put you
in Mount Everest
I'm afraid
of an avalanche
but if I
chuck you into
the Pacific Ocean
I fear a
tsunami

01, 09, 8102

在《世界语言史》
第九百六十万平方公页
看到一行字
娘炮（存目）

01, 09, 8102

On square page nine million six hundred and thousand
In *The History of World Languages*
I saw a line of characters
Niang Pao[5] (kept on file for reference)

---

5 In Chinese, it's " 娘炮 ", approximately translated as a 'Nancy boy' or 'gay' –
the translator's note.

强拆

鸟叫了一夜
早晨起来
六只麻雀站在窗台上
雀视耽耽

像要找我拼命
老妻叽咕
这些鸟胆子真大
我嘴上没说

心中明白
它们是被逼急了
昨天老屋捉漏
我端了它们老窝

Forcible removal

Birds have been chirping all night
When I rose in the morning
I saw six sparrows standing on the windowsill
Staring

As if they were going to risk their lives fighting with me
My old wife was mumbling
About their being so bold
Although I kept mum

Knowing very well
That they were being cornered
As the old house was leaking yesterday
After I removed their old nest

送葬

的人每人拿着一根香
正低头往前走

孝子却抱着死者
相片走在后面

后面有人扯嗓子喊
嗨嗨嗨

你们怎么
走到死人前头啦

At the funeral

Everyone was taking an incense
Walking ahead, with their heads lowered

The filial son, though, was holding the photo
Of the dead and walked behind them

Someone was yelling at the top of his voice:
Hey, hey, hey

What's going on?
Why are you walking ahead of the dead?

结果

四月初两个朋友来访
院里的桃
开了一树繁花

我答应
等桃熟了
给他们一人送一袋

到五月发现
只结了十七个果
后来又逐渐掉了六个

剩下的
一个被鸟啄了
一个里面生了虫

Come to fruition

Two friends came to visit in early April
The peach trees in the courtyard
Were filled with flowers

I promised to them
That I'd give them a bag each
When the peaches were ripe

By May I found
There were an additional seventeen peaches
Although six had dropped, one by one, later on

Of what remained
One was pecked by the birds
And the other, wormed through

！

早晨
伟大的夜晚
太阳照
耀出黑色的光
如雪
在空中燃烧
似火
在地下
结冰

!

Morning
Great night
The sun shows
In black light
Like snow
Burning in the air
Like fire
Freezing
Underground

一把镰刀

子夜 我睡不着
仿佛听见黑暗中声声叹息

白天清理柴房
看见一把镰刀躺在墙角
那把镰刀 ------
我用它割过羊草
父亲用它收割过稻麦

遗弃了几十年的镰刀
锈迹斑斑
像父亲脸上老年斑
刀刃上豁口
像父亲掉了牙裂开嘴巴

我俯身把镰刀扶起
像扶起病榻上老父
我用疼痛把镰刀重新擦亮
像擦亮父亲灰暗脸膛

熠熠生光镰刀
挂在墙上
夜夜照着我书房！

A sickle

At midnight   I couldn't fall asleep
As if I was listening to the sighs in the darkness

During the day when I was sorting things out in the firewood room
I saw a sickle lying in a corner
The sickle—
That I had used to cut the guinea grass
And that Father had used to reap in the rice and wheat

The sickle, abandoned for decades
Was now stained with rust
Like the age spots
And where the blade was chipped
It looked like Father's grinning mouth with fallen teeth

I bent to put the sickle up
The way I held my old father up in his sickbed
With pain, I wiped the sickle till it shone
As if I was wiping Father's grey face till it shone

Shining, the sickle
Hanging on the wall
Lighting up my study every night!

药罐

一只药罐
在火炉上
痛苦地呻吟
每天把一肚子苦水
熬成半碗眼泪

病中母亲
就这样
在生活火炉上
被命运熬成
一味苦药

The herbal clay pot

A herbal clay pot
Was moaning in pain
On the stove
Stewing a bellyful of bitter water
Into half a pot of tears every day

Mother, when sick
Was thus
Stewed into a bitter medicine
By fate
On the stove of life

空巢

她每天和自己影子
一起散步
一起晒太阳

儿子在两千里外的西北
老伴去了另一个世界
孤独与寂寞像两条纠缠的长蛇
心像一幢搬光了家具的楼房

她用儿子寄来的燕窝喂狗
让狗陪她说话
思念象一把兰州拉面
越拉越长

Empty nest

Every day she walks
With her own shadow
Sunning with it, too

Her son is in the north-west, two thousand kilometers away
Whose wife has gone to another world
Loneliness and solitude, like two entwined snakes
And the heart, a building whose furniture is all removed

She feeds her dog with the bird's nest her son has mailed her
And she gets her dog to keep her company, to talk to
Her longing, like a handful of Lanzhou pull noodle
The more you pull it, the longer it becomes...

阿弥陀佛

地铁上
一位漂亮女子
坐在爱心专座上
念千字经文

一位老人
抓住冰凉把手
低下身子问
姑娘　你念什么经？
女子瞟了一眼
继续念她经

一个刹车
老人摔倒在地上
乘客惊呼
我急忙把他扶起
他说了一声
阿弥陀佛！

一位老妇起身让座
念经的还在念经

Amitabha

On the subway
A pretty woman
Sat on a Love Seat, specially reserved for the old or disabled
And reading
A thousand-character *Earth Store Bodhisattva*

An old man
Grabbing hold of the ice-cold handle
And lowering himself said
Girl   what are you reading?
The girl glanced at him
And went on to read her classic

A sudden brake
And the old man fell onto the floor
The other passengers cried in surprise
I helped him up in a hurry
As he said
Amitabha!

An old woman rose to give him the seat
And the reader of the classic was still reading it

磨刀

他心里有个
像绳子一样的死结
越抽越紧——

蹶着屁股
磨着一把刀
头越磨越低
屁股越蹶越高
刀口露出了寒光

刚好
一个恨了几十年的人走过
他冲出院门
被篱笆桩拽住了衣裳
他听见衣襟撕裂的声音

他犹豫了一下
急忙把刀藏好

Sharpening the knife

There was a dead knot
Like a rope, in his heart
The more he pulled it the tighter it got—

His bum in the air
He was sharpening a knife
The more he sharpened it, the lower he held his head
As his bum got higher
The mouth of the knife revealed a chilling light

Just then
A man who he had been hating for decades went past
He rushed out of the gate of his courtyard
When the fence caught his clothes
And he heard the ripping of his lapel

He hesitated for a second
Then he hid away the knife

初冬

屋后香樟树
有时落下一二片
有时老半天也不掉

地上香樟叶
枯的枯
黄的黄

陈老太门前
有时三五天也不见一个人进出
有时一天会有许多人来去

今天
香樟树一直没掉
陈老太门前
有许多人进出

进进出出
有的在高声打手机
有的在低声抽泣

Early winter

The camphor tree behind the house
Sometimes has one or two leaves falling
And at other times, not a single one for a long time

The camphor tree leaves on the ground
Withered
Or yellowed

Outside the door of Granny Chen
Sometimes for three or five days, not a single one goes in or out
Sometimes, on a single day, there are many coming and going

Today
The tree does not have a single leaf fallen

And at Granny Chen's door
Many are coming and going

Going and coming
Some are calling in a loud voice on their mobile phones
And others are weeping, in a low voice

等

这个世界总在等
房价 股票 利息
有人等涨 有人等跌
婚姻 医院 学校
有人等进去 有人等出来
等一下 等一会 等一等
有人等存钱 有人等取钱
有人等下雨 有人等雨停
等人 等车 等船 等飞机
等开会等指示等通知等验收
等下班等加薪等升迁等吃饭等发财

等等等等
等到头发白
等到死
还得等火化

Waiting

This world has always been waiting

Housing price   shares   interest

Some are waiting for a rise   some, for a loss

Marriage   hospitals   schools

Some are waiting to get in   some, to get out

Wait a bit   wait a little   wait and wait

Some are waiting to deposit the money   some, to withdraw it

Some, for the rain   some, for the rain to stop

Waiting for people   for cars   for boats   for airplanes

Waiting for meetings, instructions, notices, and waiting for acceptance

Waiting to get off work for a rise in salary for a promotion for a meal

for making a fortune

Wait, wait, wait, wait

Wait till one's hair grows grey

Wait till one dies

But one still has to wait for cremation

痴呆老人

父亲被人嗤笑一生
丧葬那天
儿子让他风光一回

妻子瘫痪八年
他端饭端尿端了八年
孙子小学六年
他在校门口风里雨里等过六年

后来　他不会穿衣了
衣服只穿一只袖子
裤子把前面穿到后面

再后来　他把自己弄丢
家里人不知道他在那里

回来那天
他浮在芦苇荡里

The old man suffering from senile dementia

Father was laughed at all his life
Till the day of his burial
When his son let him have the day of his life

His wife was paralysed for eight years
He served her for that length, bringing her meals and removing her piss
The grandson attended school for six years
He spent that long waiting for him at the entrance in the wind and rain

Later on   he didn't know how to put on his clothes
Wearing only one sleeve
And his pants backwards

Still later on   he lost himself
And no one in the family knew where he had gone

On the day he came back
He was floating in the reeds

这些人那些人

上世纪 80 年代初
那些年轻人穿着喇叭裤
提着录音机
在大街上唱歌跳舞
完全不顾老年人感受！

本世纪初开始
这些老年人
每天晚上在公园里
广场上唱歌跳舞
完全不顾年轻人感受！

经仔细观察
发现
这些人
其实都是 40 年前的
那些人

These ones, those ones

In the 1980s
Those young ones, in their bell-bottoms
Carried their tape-recorders
Singing and dancing on the streets
Totally ignoring how the old felt!

In the beginning of this century
These old ones
Dance and sing on the square
Of the park every evening
Totally ignoring how the young feel!

But if you look at them more carefully
You'll see
That these ones
Are actually those ones
Who grew up 40 years ago

在乡下

一个漂亮女人
急匆匆钻进稀树丛

褪下裤子
别以为她有神经病

即使她露出了两瓣白屁股
也别以为她要偷情

其实这是
一个内急的女人

在乡下一个内急的女人
会不管不顾

In the country

A pretty woman
Went into a thin bush in a great hurry

She took off her pants
Don't take her as someone gone mad

Even if she has revealed two halves of a white bum
It doesn't mean that she is fucking with someone by stealth

In actual fact
She is a woman urgently answering the call

In the country when a woman urgently answers the call of nature
She'll do it anyway, regardless

退休后

回到家乡发现
老年活动室

设在当年
我们一年级的教室

许多同学像上学一样
每天都会去坐坐

那天我一进去
班长拍拍旁边座位

来——来——
还按小时候位子坐

In my retirement

When I went back to my hometown I found
That the Activity Room for the Elderly People

Was located in the Grade-I Classroom
Of my old primary school

Many of my old classmates would go there
And sit for a while, like in the old days

The other day, as soon as I got in
Class Monitor patted on the seat next to me and said

Come – come
Do it as you did, like when you were still a child

断刺

晚饭后
舌头在牙缝抠出一根
半寸长的刺

妻举着这细东西
家里好几天没吃鱼了
你嘴里咋会有刺?

于是给妈妈看
妈妈在灯下端详了好久
认定是鱼刺

老妻还是不信
洗好碗
又拿去给邻居看

我也是事后才想起
昨天中午
有人约饭在外面吃刀鱼

The broken fishbone

After dinner
My tongue picked from between my teeth
A fishbone half an inch long

My wife, raising the thin thing:
We haven't had fish for many days
But how did you get that into your mouth?

Then we showed it to Mom
She examined it under the lamp for a long time
And identified it as a fishbone

My old wife, unconvinced
Did the dishes
And took it to a neighbour to see

And it was not till afterwards that I recalled
I had eaten a knife fish at a lunch I was invited to
Yesterday noon

农家·乐

五十多岁的单身王老板
经营一爿农家乐

他每天上山下河
挖竹笋摘野菜捞鱼

回来往厨房一放
对客人说

凉拌热炒清蒸红烧
你们随意

然后屁颠屁颠
去找搭子叉麻将

Rural•Happiness

Boss Wang, single, aged 50
Runs a Rural Happy restaurant

Daily, he heads for the hills or goes down to the river
And brings back bamboo shoots, wild vegetables and fish

He puts these in the kitchen
And says to his customers

I can make cold salad, stir-fry, steam or braise them
To your heart's content

Then he, so happy
Goes to find his Mahjong mates

告慰

祭祖化锡箔时
有几只元宝跳出火盆
满地翻滚

我追着去捡
每一次刚要抓到
却又滚走

妈妈说：别抢别抢
都有都有
翻滚的元宝立时停了下来

Comforting

When sacrifices were offered to the ancestors and tin foils were being burnt
A few ingots jumped out of the firepan
Rolling about on the ground

I gave them a chase
But each time I was about to get them
They rolled away

Mom said: Don't, don't
Everyone will have them
The rolling ingots stopped at once

二十五史

战乱 逃荒 解放 合作社 炼钢
人民公社 亩产超万斤（虚报） 吃大食堂
分田到户 农转居 新农村

读遍二十四史
翻烂春秋
没发现有关丰收村文字

查县志 乡志
也找不到任何记载
丰收村的猪丝牛迹

我们村的历史
是由九十六岁的小满
婆婆口述

Twenty-four histories

Wars   famine   liberation   collectives   steelmaking
People's Commune   10,000 *jin* produced in one *mu* (false)   eating at a big
                                                                    canteen
Fields divided by households   peasant-to-resident status   new villages

After I read all the twenty-four histories
Till springs and autumns went rotting
I did not find anything written about Bumper Crop Village

I checked the county annals and the village annals
And still could find nothing on record
Not even a spider's trace of it about Bumper Crop Village

The history of our village
Was orally related by the granny, aged 96
Of Xiao Man

父亲的烟斗

整理旧物
发现一只
父亲用过的烟斗

我磕磕烟斗
掉出来
粗的像榆树叶
细的是玉米的流苏

划亮火柴
一股辛辣
呛出两眼泪水
几点火星里
父亲咳嗽　咯血的面容
闪现了一下

四周空空荡荡
我把烟斗与内疚
装进一只小盒

My father's pipe

When I went through what remained of the old things
I found
A pipe my father had used

I knocked it
When something dropped
Something thick like an elm tree leaf
And something thin, like the fringe of a corn

When I struck a match
I smelled something pungent
I got choked and shed tears

In the sparks
Flashed Father's coughing
His blood-coughing face

It's hollow and empty all around
I put the pipe and guilt
In a small box

拜佛的潮女

低胸衫很低
珠光俗气
她把点燃的香插进香炉
在莆团上跪下
叩头
一对大奶脱衫而出
像供奉菩萨的
两个白馒头

The fashionable woman worshipping Buddha

In a low-cut blouse, very low
All jewelry
She put the burning incense in the incense burner
And knelt down on the cushion
Kowtowing
As her breasts popped out of her blouse
Like two white steamed buns
Offered at the altar for Buddha

九月初九

夜已睡了很久
他还在喝酒

对面墙上他的影子
如他的日子一般寂寞孤独

他不断给影子敬酒
影子摇摇晃晃　不懂世故

倒是桌下的一声猫叫
引出了他一阵大笑

这一天是九月初九
几个酒瓶歪在他的脚下
流出几滴辛辣的泪

Ninth of Nine

The night, long asleep
He was still drinking

His shadow on the opposite wall
As lonely and solitary as his days

He kept toasting the shadow
The shadow kept shaking   not knowing the human ways

But it's the cat underneath the table
That induced him to laughter

That was Ninth of Nine
A number of bottles lay askew at his foot
A few drops of hot water running out of them

拾废者

一辆三轮车
在深巷里 转
装满废塑料
旧报纸 破衣服

他把别人废弃的日子
堆在太阳路过的窗下
想堆成一座金字塔

The scavenger

Riding a tricycle
he was going the rounds   in deep lanes
The tricycle filled with plastic waste
Old newspapers   worn clothes

He put the days abandoned by the others
In a heap outside a window that the sun went past
Hoping to heap it up to a pyramid of gold

四个老婆

从外面回家
路过村口
看见老婆与一堆女人
聊得起劲
开门时发现忘带钥匙
折回去跟她要
走到身后
我叫了声：老婆
有四个女人一齐回答
"哎——"

Four wives

When I came home from outside
Past the mouth of the village
I saw my wife chatting, energetically
With a crowd of women
It's not till I tried to open the door when I realised I didn't have the key
So I went back to ask her for it
As I got behind her
I called out: Lao Po (old woman or wife)
Four women answered in unison:
'Aye—'

感觉

男人常年不着家
她感觉像个寡妇
逛完公园出来
看见小男孩手里透明气球棒
突然感觉想要了
一路上感觉今天遇到
男人都很有感觉
急匆匆赶回家
感觉很饿
吃了棍子面包和香肠
却越吃越饿
又把一根黄瓜搓了又搓洗了又洗
在滴滴答答流水声中
总感觉从没感觉的
离婚老王在对门喊她

The feeling

With her man constantly away from home
She felt like a widow
When she finished her walk in the park
She saw the transparent balloon stick in the hand of a little boy
And suddenly felt like wanting it
On her way she had a feeling that all the men
She met were handsome
She hurried home
Feeling hungry
She finished off a stick bread and a sausage
But the more she ate the hungrier she got
So she took a cucumber, scrubbing it and washing it
And in the drip-drop sound of the flowing water
She had a feeling that the divorced Old Wang opposite her
Was calling her although she'd never had a feel for him

飙语

三十多年前
从上海坐火车
一路北上
在绿皮车厢
掠过的白墙上
总能看到
人定胜天
横扫一切牛鬼蛇神
人有多大胆　地
有多大产
千万不要
忘记阶级斗争
少生孩子多养猪
文攻武卫
这样的标语
那天去浦江
城市广场溪林小馆
发现这些老
标语
用红色烤在一只只
白搪瓷小茶杯上
但"武功再好也怕菜刀"
这一条
以前没见过

Slogans

Thirty-odd years ago
I went by train in Shanghai
All the way north
On the white walls
The green-skinned compartment swept across
One could always see
Such slogans as
'Man Will Overcome the Sky'
'Make a Clean Sweep of All the Cow-devils and Snake-spirits'
'The Output of the Fields is Matched by the Boldness of Human Beings'
'Never Forget the Class Struggle'
'Produce More Kids than Pigs'
'Words to Attack and Weapons for Defence'
The other day when I went to Pujiang
In Creek Forest Small Restaurant
I found these old
Slogans
Burnt in red
Onto small
Enameled cups
But there was one
Slogan that I had never seen before:
'Even the best martial artist is afraid of the kitchen knife'

埋单

羊毛出
在猪身上
狗埋单

狗毛出
在猪身上
羊埋单

猪毛出
在羊身上
狗埋单

狗毛出在羊
身上
猪埋单

羊毛出在狗
身上猪
埋单

羊毛出在羊身上
猪不埋单
狗跑了

狗毛长在人身上
谁
埋单？

Footing the bills

Sheep's hair comes
From the pig
The dog foots the bill

The dog's hair comes
From the pig
The sheep foot the bill

The pig's hair comes
From the sheep
The dog foots the bill

The dog's hair comes
From the sheep
The pig foots the bill

The sheep's hair comes from the
Dog the pig
Foots the bill

The sheep's hair comes from the sheep
The pig doesn't foot the bill
The dog runs away

When the dog's hair comes from a human being
Who
Foots the bill?

信仰

因你理佛
我不再对迷信有微词

儿子知道
妈妈是一个有信仰的人

坚信儿女给不了的
佛能给你

但妈妈可能还不知道
儿子也是一个有信仰的人

坚信
佛

给不了你的
我会给你

Belief

Because you believe in Buddhism
I no longer criticize it

My son knows
That Mom is a woman who believes

Firmly convinced that whatever sons and daughters can't give you
Buddha can give

But Mom may not know
That her son is also a man who believes

Convinced
That whatever Buddha

Can't give you
I can give

存款

在废品收购站
小满婆婆从
比她年轻许多的
女人手里接过
九枚三元六角镍币
用皱巴巴的手绢
包好装进一只塑料袋
解开外裤翻开线裤
存进两腿三角区
这里缝着一个小口袋
那是她的私人银行

The deposit

In the salvage station
Xiao Man's Granny took
9 nickel coins to the amount of 3.60 yuan
From the hands of women
Much younger than her
And wrapped them up with a crumpled handkerchief
In a plastic bag
She opened her outer pants and the woolen pants underneath
And put it in the triangle between her legs
There, a tiny pocket was sewn in
That was her private bank

10000 年 1 月 1 日

太阳从西边升起
企鹅还在火星斗地主
鳖从月球乘飞
鸡去给黄鼠狼拜年
七千九百八
十四岁的阿尔法狗
从喜马拉雅海沟出发
翻过马里亚纳雪山
在炎热的南极
聚集地宫六千号
参加梵蒂冈、璃鲁、图瓦鲁
圣马力诺、列支敦斯
塞舌尔、圣基茨和尼维斯
七国金土豆会议
谈起曾于公元 2017 年与
人类的李世石、柯杰
下围棋
尽管被赶不走拍不灭的
飞象咬的全铁都是
黑洞仍满是自豪
一万年太久
只争朝夕

On 1 January, 10000

The sun rises in the West
Penguins are still fighting the landlords on Mars
Freshwater turtles take flight from the moon
Chickens pay their New Year's visit to the weasels
In 7980
Alpha Dog, 14
Departs the Himalayan Trench
Climbs the snow mountains of Mariana
And, in the hot South Pole
Gathers Land Palace No. 6000
He attends the 7-Nation Gold Potato Conference
Jointly run by Vatican, Nauru, Tuvalu
San Marino, Lichtenstein
Seychelles, St Kitts and Nevis
Talking about him
Having a go
With Li Shishi and Ke Jie, from the human world
In 2017
Although the Black Hole
Remains fully proud
Bitten by the flying elephant
That refuses to be driven off and destroyed
Ten thousand years are too long
Seize the day

机关·枪

1
自进了机关
我一直在缝防弹衣
机关里有一把枪
比手枪射程远
比步枪火力猛
机关里的枪是机关枪

2
长期蹲在机关里
并没有看见枪
却发现有子弹飞来飞去
有时会被莫名其妙流弹击伤
有时羡慕嫉妒恨枪托
把人砸得鲜血直趟

3
机关枪有机关
在机关蹲久了
如摸不到枪机关
难免会成为别人的枪
射出的子弹
有时会打在自己身上

4
机关枪有时藏在嘴里
有时架在纸上
有人冲你笑

可能上天 也可能入地
笔管里一粒粒子弹
能让胸前开会
也能让名誉立刻身亡

The *Jiguan*•Gun[6]

1

Since I got into the *jiguan* (work unit)
I have been sewing my bullet-proof vest
In the *jiguan*, there is a gun
With a shooting range further than the pistol
With firepower more violent than a rifle
The gun in the *jiguan* is a *jiguan* gun

2

Squatting in a *jiguan* for a long time
I have never seen a pistol
Although I find bullets flying
Sometimes I get wounded by a stray bullet for no reason at all
Sometimes I envy, I'm jealous of, I hate the gunstock
As it can smash one till one bleeds

3

The *jiguan* gun has a *jiguan*[7]
If you squat for a long time in the *jiguan*
And cannot find the *jiguan* of a gun
You may become the bullet
Shot out of the gun of someone else
And the bullet may hit your own body

---

6 " 机 关 枪 " (jiguan qiang) means 'machine guns'. But " 机 关 " can also mean 'work units', which is why the poet puts a dot between the 'work units' and 'guns' (枪) 。
7 " 机关 " (jiguan) can also mean 'mechanism'.

4

The *jiguan* gun sometimes hides in the mouth

Sometimes it is put on the paper

When someone smiles for you

You may go to heavens   or you may go underground

The pen tube contains bullets

That can hold meetings on one's chest

Or cause instant death to honour

雪山驼掌

城市 K 字街头
迎面走来一头骆驼
驮着戈壁
驮着祁连山

当年在祁连
我驮着土豆
驮着书本
走向一座山村小学

骆驼向东
我往北
交错而过
彼此望了一眼

于市北聚餐
面对敦煌楼名菜：
雪山驼掌
我拿起筷子
又放下

The Snow Mountain Camel Hooves

On Street K in the city
There came headlong a camel
Carrying the Gebi Desert and the Qilian Mountains
On its back

In the old days when I was in Qilian
I carried potatoes
And books
As I walked towards a primary school in a mountain village

As the camel walked east
I walked north
When we went past
We looked at one another

I had dinner in the city north
And faced a famous dish in Dunhuang Pavilion:
Snow Mountain Camel Hooves
As soon as I picked up my chopsticks
I put them down

晒

母亲晒被子
顺便晒自己

被子晒醒了
母亲却睡着了

晒醒的被子
像母亲一样贴心

睡着的母亲
比被子还温暖

Sunning

Mother was sunning the quilt
As well as herself

The quilt was sunned alive
While Mother fell asleep

The quilt, awake
Was as caring as Mother

And Mother, asleep
Was warmer than the quilt

师姐

投票前她对我说
你投我我投你
争取两人一起去

给她投好票
才知道
她把票投给了自己

这是一九七五年
她去了七二一工人大学
我留在车间磨凸轮

一九九三年
我回到上海做公务员
她在兰州下了岗

二〇一五年某日
旅游寄宿南通海安
突然见她在老家电视上

跳广场舞
我想再给她投一票
无奈摇控器不能当投票器

Sister by trade

Before casting the vote I said to her:
If you vote me, I'll vote you
We'll try to go together

It was not till after I cast the vote
That I realized
She had voted herself

That was 1975
When she went to July 21st Workers University
And I stayed behind in the workshop grinding the cams

In 1993
When I came back to Shanghai to work as a civil servant
She was laid off in Lanzhou

One day in 2015
When I stayed for the night in Hai'an, Nantong, on a tourist trip
I suddenly saw her on the TV screen in her own hometown

Dancing the public square dance
I was thinking of casting a vote for her
But, unfortunately, my remote couldn't do the trick

过桥

一个小老汉
一辆破三轮
一车正广泉

小老汉蹬着正广泉
正广泉坐着三轮车
三轮车与桥坡较劲

进退　　进退
欲进一轮
却退半轮

我站在二楼窗前
用力一推
三轮车一下上了桥

他下桥时
我使劲
拽着窗框

Crossing the Bridge

A small old man
A broken tricycle
Full of AQUARIUS

While the small old man was riding his tricycle
The AQUARIUS was sitting in it
The tricycle was battling against the bridge slope

Up-down   up-down
One wheel up
Half-wheel down

I stood on the second floor in front of the window
And gave him a powerful push
The tricycle went on the bridge at once

When he went down the bridge
I forcibly grabbed
The window frame

阿姨山下

从夏河县城去拉卜楞寺
不到一公里
路上有雪
　　雪上有血
朝圣者把藏袍
两只袖子
　　系腰部
每走三步
双手举过头顶
伸展合十匍匐在地
他们背对我
站起来
低于贡唐宝塔
扑下去高于三千
六百八十米的阿姨山

At the foot of the Ayi Mountains

From Xiahe county to Labrang Monastery
it was less than one kilometer
there was blood on the road
    blood on the snow
the pilgrims tied the two sleeves
of their Tibetan gown
    around their waists
every three steps they took
they would raise their hands above their heads
extending them, putting their palms together and went down on all fours
they stood up
with their backs towards me
lower than the Gongtang Pagoda
but when they threw themselves down on the ground they were taller than
the Ayi Mountains 3680 metres high

女儿女儿

暑假里
女儿给女儿
报书法
围棋
钢琴唱歌
绘画
玫瑰小作家
兴趣班
我问女儿女儿
最喜欢上什么课
她说我
最喜欢上下课

Daughter, Daughter

During the summer holiday
My daughter, on her daughter's account
Applied for entry to calligraphy classes
Go classes
Piano classes, singing classes
Painting classes
Rose children's writers classes
Interest classes
When I asked my daughter's daughter
What're her favourite classes
She said that her
Most favourite classes were no classes

"牛氓"

1974 年 3 月 5 日
他在决心书结尾写道:
"我一定要操她"
被厂部叫去问话
"这是你真实想法吗?"
"是!请看我实际行动"
第 3 天,他被当作流氓
遣送回原籍监督劳动
因姓牛
此后人们一直叫他牛氓
也有人叫他牛盲
3 个月后他想操 的那个
女劳模与厂长儿子结婚
10 年后他开五金厂
现在牛氓企业准备上市
记者让这个很牛的盲
谈创业经历经验
他说:当年把"超"错写成"操"
我这一切都是
"操"出来的

A 'Knave'

On 5 March 1974

He wrote at the end of a statement of determination:

'I must *cao* her'[8]

As a result, he was questioned by the factory department

'Is that what you are really thinking of doing?'

'Yes! Please see my real action'

On the 4th day, he was regarded as a knave

And repatriated to his ancestral home town for supervised labour

Because his surname was Niu,[9] people called him Niumang[10]

There were also people who called him Niumang[11]

3 months subsequently   the one he wanted to cao

A model worker, married the son of the factory director

10 years after, he ran a hardware factory

And his Niumang business was ready to be listed

When a reporter interviewed this blind bull

About his entrepreneurial experience

He said: back then I got it wrong by turning " 超 " into " 操 "[12]

Thus caofucking

Everything up

---

8 Among its many meanings, the word 'cao' (操) means 'to fuck' – the translator's note.

9 Or "牛" , meaning a cow or bull or ox – the translator's note.

10 'Niumang' (牛 氓) , a homonym with 'liumang' (流 氓) , a knave or rascal – the translator's note.

11 'Niumang' (牛盲) , a homonym with 'liumang' (流氓) – the translator's note.

12 " 超 "(chao) into" 操 "(cao), the first means to surpass or overtake, and the second means to fuck – the translator's note.

赶苍蝇

商场门口
她会放电眼
正对着你

遮去三点的火辣身材
磁铁一样
吸住许多暧昧目光

一只苍蝇飞来
停在两腿间一点
他伸手去赶

后面人一挤
戳开一个洞

那女人一声不
吭

Whisking the flies off

In front of the department store
She, facing you
Would flash her electric eyes

Her hot body, with three spots covered up
Would attract many dubious glances
Like a magnet

A fly came flying
And stopped between her legs
He stuck out his hand to whisk it off

People crowded up from behind
A hole was poked open

The woman didn't utter a single
Sound

对话

套间里
沙发在对椅子发话

茶壶最近话太多
衣架现在已挂不住东西

那个摇头扇
摇过去后再没转过来

保险箱
已藏不住秘密

衣柜里那件睡袍
破了

椅子回答：明白
我去办

A conversation

In the suite
A sofa was talking with a chair

The teacups were so talkative these days
The clothes hangers can't even hang anything

The head-shaking fan
Refuses to come back when its head is shaken

The safe
Can no longer hide the secrets

The pajamas in the wardrobe
Got a hole in it

The chair said: Point taken
Will go and fix them up

奇怪

保洁工刘阿姨
回家神秘地对老公说

今天去会议室清扫
一开门就听见

那些桌子椅子
饮水机、茶叶罐、盆栽

肖主席的书法
丁院长的国画在开会

那个扩音器
讲的话

我只听出一句饭局
也可能是范局

其它的
都没听懂

刘阿姨讲完
发现老公满头是汗

Strange

Ayi Liu, a cleaner
Mysteriously, said to her husband when getting home

When I went to do the cleaning in the meeting room
I heard, as soon as I opened the door

The desks, the chairs
The water dispenser, the tea cans, the potted plants

Calligraphy by Party Secretary Xiao
And traditional Chinese paintings by Director Ding were all having a
meeting

What the loudspeaker
Was talking about

I could only make out two words: Fanju （饭局） [13]
Though it could be Fanju （范局） [14]

I didn't understand
The rest of it

When Ayi Liu finished
She found that her husband's forehead was sweating all over

_____

13 Appointed meals. – the translator's note.
14 Just a meaningless homonym with the above one, pronounced the same as 'fanju', a meaningless word – the translator's note.